Violent Blues

Also by Bruce Willard

Holding Ground

ViOLEnt BLUES

Bruce Willard

Four Way Books
Tribeca

Please direct all inquiries to:
Editorial Office
Four Way Books
POB 535, Village Station
New York, NY 10014
www.fourwaybooks.com

Library of Congress Cataloging-in-Publication Data

Names: Willard, Bruce, author.
Title: Violent blues / Bruce Willard.
Description: New York, NY : Four Way Books, [2016] | Includes bibliographical references.
Identifiers: LCCN 2016007102 | ISBN 9781935536758 (softcover : acid-free paper)
Classification: LCC PS3623.I5534 A6 2016 | DDC 811/.6--dc23
LC record available at http://lccn.loc.gov/2016007102

This book is manufactured in the United States of America and printed on acid-free paper.

Four Way Books is a not-for-profit literary press. We are grateful for the assistance
we receive from individual donors, public arts agencies, and private foundations.

This publication is made possible with public funds from the New York State Council on the Arts,
a state agency.

[clmp]

We are a proud member of the Community of Literary Magazines and Presses.

Distributed by University Press of New England
One Court Street, Lebanon, NH 03766

CONTENTS

*. . . each of us
joins night's ongoing story
wherever night overtakes him,
the heart astonished to find belonging
and thanks answering thanks*
                        —Li-Young Lee

i.

EVEN

All day the wind scrambled the trees,
sky-shapes I could not have imagined
if not for the passing front. At night,
the breaking of small branches,
pencil chatter of bones across the roof.
When I woke even the sky was blue.

FALL

. . .What did you come here for if not to hear
Finality in the soft click of a latch
                                    —Larry Levis

I turned back each clock one hour
one hour before bed. Even
the thermostat—eye
in a hall of closed doors—
resting better now, its work
fully measured for the time

being. Nothing more
than the tick of morning
trying to catch up
and fill the cold space
behind every door.

THE CALLING

Sometimes at dusk when the earth gives its sweet breath to the trees,
I think how I took a stranger's life and whispered not
so much as his name to the asphalt sky.

How each year, on my mother's birthday, I hear the warbled rasp
of his breathing, and it pushes and draws me like a blues harp
soaked in whiskey from which the bent yawl of reeds
becomes the song I have to play.

Biking that night, decades ago, I felt the desert wind coming over the ridge
meeting the November valley air. Spermy smell of fennel and ceanothus.
Past oak and manzanita. Past cereus and chaparral grass.
Past the cornering lanes. Past the houses I mistook for home.
Past the church at Mt Carmel with its weathered perfection.

If I was drawn to him, no line was visible. There were no lines.
Just a mountain road, uphill tick of my pedaling.
His downhill whir of speed, sound of his nylon jacket flapping.
Click of handlebars, crush of steel and skull.

Beside the road where he lay, an owl called. *Listen,*
I thought. And I heard how its voice survives each question,
how each question survives the shadow of clouds.
And I called to my stranger that I might hear his voice,
knowing not even his name. I called to him and he became
to me like wind on a flagpole, wind in a tree, something
moving that can never be moved.

WHAT WORKS

I try to understand
what makes things work

sometimes I can't
separate love from making

sometimes work makes love
trying   sometimes works

in un-understandable ways

I love what I can't understand
          I work to separate

the things   I love
to make   trying
sometimes

PUZZLE

I'm working to put together the pieces
from a box with no cover photo.
Trying, by memory,
each shape and color.

Some of the pieces are bent
or chewed, and one, at least, is used
to shim a clock that ticks
fast-slow, fast-slow, fast-slow.

A grand and violent landscape,
no people for reference.
White and black fence
lines. Uncrossable.

Overwhelmed by drifts.

JANUARY BUS RIDE

Town feels close to night.
Pattern of cross streets,

dip-rhythm of blocks.
Every view through gauzy

windows looks like home:
TV-blues, flash of late

sun wicking higher,
diminishing possibility of stars.

Wet, rubber shoes,
closing of doors; passengers

transferring one stop
to the next. Soon

is the hour I could board
almost any bus

and say the route leads home.

MGB

Mine was a kind of red,
burnt orange by the sun,
each year paler than the year before.
No one's started on demand.
There was no reason,
no predicting. May afternoons,

left at the Wash N' Fold,
past Cow Shit Corner,
where the manure was warmed,
mixed by late-morning,
with the ocean air. Or right,
down Maine Street,
past the fishermen, drunk
by noon, refusing

to shift from second to third
for fear of losing the familiar
hold-back rumble between
acceleration and exhaust,
past the girls at Frosty's,
across the bridge by the mill,
not yet 4, the time when the factories let out,
when the weekend begins

in earnest, and everything
worth waiting for is just ahead,
around the bend,
within cruising range,

the alluring paleness
of sky so white
you could almost feel the night, moonrise
over the growing fields

and farms with their junkyard
dreams of vehicles
in barns and culverts;
in each house the graduate shadows
stripping color
from the impossible finish.

MOTU

I couldn't, shouldn't, have wanted
so much rain. Night, rolling
swells from the north across the lagoon,
wave upon wave, wave on reef,
wave-spray over thatched roof, no one
to tell one from the next.

And did you know it would rain?
I did.
And did you expect the wind?
I did.
*And did you want it in a way
you cannot bear to admit?*
I cannot bear it.

What will you do?
I will choose words.
What kind of words?
Words that stand for rain—

as when morning clears
and full white clouds pass
over the lagoon and night
soaks in, setting roots
at the first sign of sun.

PROGRESSIVE

I fail progressively.
Forget the names of people,
birds, flowers, clouds.
I forget the names
of songs. *Presence before precision*, my way
of saying *words for words, sound
movement for loss.*

I fail my fear,
become still,
still in love
with my children
who no longer know me,
my wife whose naked body
slides through my arms.

The seasons run together
as in irrigated western towns
with a history of thirst
and hangover. And joy
becomes the habit it was meant
to be, contentment,
for which no season's
name is known.

THE MIDDLE GROUND

The teacher met me inside the school gates
on middle ground. *We've noticed bruises*
on your son's arms and legs, she said.
And there were no words
I could say to express my self: a single father,
the implicated guilt, forty years of it
rising from the small winter inside me, closing
my throat, my tongue
curling like a frostbit leaf
past the color of its rage.

And I made a sound, I think, like a ship
getting underway, something inevitable and true,
irrespective of the darkness of the water around me,
a sound defiant and pure as metaphor
with no referent, love with no hailing port,
a sound like a propeller churning phosphorus and ragweed,
water moving steadily under the hull
away from shallow ground,
past ledges, to deeper water.

SELF-PORTRAIT

A scratch in the finish,
not deep, not long.
A tick in the record's refrain.
A song that drafts,
held off by the wind,
the smoke that circles again.

ii.

REVISION

Mid-February revealed in red: correction,
cardinal, blister, rose, store-front
heart, snow sunset, scarlet
lingerie on white skin.

Lone bonsai, indoors, ever-
green edged in rust,
its limbs overreaching
its given space. Time

for pruning. Here,
close to the branches,
the quick, turned
joinery and excess.

How seasoned
these bloodless cuts,
these short and blessed days.

BREATHLESS

This morning, minus 12 degrees,
the furnace's exhaust almost vertical,
high as the spruce beside the house—
mouthy, moist braid of cumulus giving up
as little as possible to a dry and navy sky.

This morning, all things close-held.
Not a bird on the suet feeder.
No sign of plow or trash or cable
truck. Not even the small dog
peering from the porch next door.

This morning, I am thankful for all that remains—
the holidays, closed and out of view,
some large flurries floating past the window,
moisture held up in small, narrow-shouldered
drifts between each pane.

HAPTIC

I have a feeling things are heavier than they seem:
people in elevators, day lilies in rain.
I have a feeling some thing's always missing: type
longing for whiteness, a page longing for ink.

Night is tall like a church, stars ringing
from the steeple of its unweighting. Each morning:
life horizontal, freeways streaming, fog in river valleys,
train whistles two towns away.

Gravity accumulates moisture
like tears: drip of branches, flowers
shedding each small grief. Everything rising
until some dew point is reached.

They say we travel, move to the next town, vacate
to change our lives, lighten the load.
But they're wrong; weight recycles—
day on, day off.

Yesterday morning I watched snow
even the peaks of a deep mountain valley
filling chutes, covering buttresses and cliffs,
making cornices of every ridge.

So much spindrift rising, circling, settling.
Urgent its remoteness. Remote its urgency. I feel it.
What doesn't avalanche is blown away.

WATCHING CHICKADEES

Late spring, officially
two weeks past winter—
16 degrees in Grand Junction
last night. How unexpected,
to see chickadees at the feeder,
a place they expect
to return to, find sustenance
as surprise, something unearned,
a food we all desire, that knowing—
part change, part reference
to something we think is gone—
a gesture, gratuitous
as the bloody warmth of first clouds
born from the unfathomable
blues of morning.

And what did I expect?
That I might find a place
to come home to,
a flock of my species
one wing-glide away,
a sun-struck fir.
But not the seed.
Not a kernel of this.

ALOOF

I don't play the piano
these days; I keep it
like a *fake book* in the center
of my home.

I have a fire to feed
but I let it smolder.
Smoke wisps
from the chimney,
each phrase opening—clear sky,
a place the wind blows through.

There's a piece I have to play
but I don't face the music
head on. I take her from the side:
measured voice to open ear,
my mouth which cups, luffs
and makes room for song.

ONCE

From the train's window, mid-valley, a church,
it seems, dark stone, rain-soaked,
chiseled around the edges, its sides refusing entry

the way a poem might first appear,
stained glass of the heart, sun behind,
tunneling through its nave and branchy panes,

mullions like consonants, withholding
a reticent, vowelly, inner warmth
once removed but longing
to spill itself to the gunmetal ground.

INDEPENDENCE DAY

Woke up to the sound of fireworks
above the city. Boom,
rebound of some foreign joy.
10 p.m. and the house is dark
except for the report of dreams—
the way they echo
between hard objects
and make their way to sea
beyond.

TREND

we eat out more
and more often
we do not eat at home

home is less
a place we go
for sustenance

than sleep
a place to weather
the night

if we are what we make
what are we
when we make only love

and not the savory
vowel of meat
or hulled fruit

the flesh of our labored communion

THE THINNEST NOISE

When I heard how noise masks
the gaping poignancy of evening—
the TV that becomes itself,
conversation, the pump whose circulation
covers everything but the pool's mirror
image of black sky, I was ready

to let silence have her fill
of me, the clean allure of nothing
fill me with her breath—
as she fills the dome of a bell,
or the dark heart of a mailbox,

or redeems the loins of an empty pocket
with her peculiar abstinence.
And I felt my eyes go narrow and wet
and, from my throat,
the thinnest noise became

like air drawn over the instrument
of my throat, bent, raw, and proud.

EBITDA

Because I am one
part entrepreneur
I make a living
with what is missing—moving
air for the desk-bound,
clothing for the naked,
conveyance for the becalmed.

I cross the middle ground
between have and want,
firm ground and blue water,
a discretionary point
beyond ebb's mark.

Because I am one
part entrepreneur
I calculate the gross
margin of living,
length divided by distance;
earnings by interest,
time, desire, affection:

one part, a pier
whose ambition bridges
the rhetoric of shadow; the other
a ramp that rises
with the float of dream.

THE STEEL FRAMERS

How they do it I do not know,
their faith so certain
everything must stand

for strength. Where metal
meets the clouds, a place
sky comes between

their hammer blows,
the airy solitude
of their striking

arms and sound,
each cause, effect
held up by doubt.

TRAMPOLINE

Not round like the common family
variety but extended
with padded sides and deep
corners that could swallow a ball
or sweatshirt or can of beer
or break a child's fall
to middle earth. Part lawn
ornament, part call to action,
13 years ago, a present for my son
the year we merged families,
it received the weight
of us drawn together
towards some inevitable point
before catapulting us away.
Launching, cradling, regathering
our bodies with its inward pull.

Over time, we learned to take our rise
and fall alternately, boost our partner's
height, jumping in unison
to share the view. This morning,
a target for sprinklers, the Rain Bird's
flat-thatched call, ping of spray on steel,
legs longing for levity.

What pressure lifts us now?
Brings us to the peached underside
of sycamore leaves, suspends us
for a moment, wind and sun

feathering our face,
pumping our legs,
swinging our arms
clearing the fence once more.

IT DON'T MEAN A THING

When I set out for jazz
I was all about the passing note.
The way a chord might move from minor
to major with just the turn of a finger. As if
by crossing the gray area between keys
I could sustain a half-moment's flight
to somewhere more home than home.

Next it was inversions. I tried spreading
my hands. Playing underneath
the melody: a flotilla of notes
beside a departing ship, a flock
of birds leaving Damariscotta for Boothbay,
octaves from the middle pier of C.

Before the engine of bass
found its groove,
turbines thumping,

boogie of left moving
the woogie of right
for good measure,

blue notes riding
the wake of downbeat,
dieseling back and forth

as sound does
following the craft of prospect,
moving with uncertain

certainty, the controlling
uncontrolled, on course now
to some unfinished paradise.

CLEAN

I'm ready now.
In the kitchen,
on the table.
In the foyer.
In the hall
next to the laundry
over the banging
sound the washer makes
grinding its sweet, wet clean.

In my head.
In my hips.
In my heart.
What's missing
here and now.

Weathered tee,
holy jeans,
single sock
on the floor.
Quick cycle,
tumble finish.
Fold me. Pair me.
Leg to leg.
Foot to foot.
Turn me
inside out.

iii.

HEAT

This morning, late season, the sun pushing
above the trees, ever higher, melting the rime
of new snow, steam lifting it effortlessly,
rising like smoke.

No one told me, exactly, that to love another,
love anything, was to admire
what they admire,
look through the passing thing

like heat that vibrates in a sunlit window
above a radiator. How many winters
I have stood looking
out at the cold, wind

passing through branches
of fir and jack pine and not known
the movement was what I loved—

not the thing left behind.

SURF AND TURF

A friend of mine in Maine tells me the trend
on dying: burying half one's ashes,
setting the rest to drift at sea.

And I can see it now: the last supper,
the penultimate choice—steak or lobster?
My turn coming around, the big decision:

split my bet, have my cake—
death by chocolate, no doubt—
the chewy solidarity of terra firma,

benedictory icing of fine words,
some pithy, elegiac platitude
etched in stone. The other cordial,

as just as sweet and, perhaps, more
moving; ashen spirit on my lips,
the diurnal phrase catching tide,

flotsam words, making
their way to some wooded shore.

PHOTO SHOOT

I spend the day making pictures of clothes.
Not my clothes. Nor anyone's in particular.
Shirts, sweaters, and jackets
meant to have a life of their own.

We fill them with tissue, tape the arms for gesture,
give time a chance to settle every sleeve.
Afterwards, we strike clean the scene
the way winter strikes clean the ground.

How I have come to love this passing—
the stylized space of each wearable thing,
the image dispossessed
after the form recedes.

FINDINGS

On the floor near Gate 8, a button,
the kind carved of bone
from another world, free now,
perhaps, separated from its purpose,
straining to hold two pieces of fabric,
time against time, grace against pressure.

As if it were waiting for someone
or some means of conveyance.
So I slipped it into my pocket,
let it ride with coins of various value.

Added it to a Chinese bowl of findings
on my desk—memorabilia,
castoffs, the tools of my trade.
Fastened it with a hatpin to a piece of wool—
one side flannelled, the other buffed smooth
by miles of wear.

MUSSELS

A month without an "r" in it.
Without the consonance of fog
or sibilance of wind. When the smell
of rockweed rides miles in from the coast,
dissipates, returns after dark.

In the morning she asked to go musseling.
He filled the truck with shoes for black rock,
crates—blue and slotted—for keepers,
two wide-brimmed hats to hold off the sun.

They hiked to the place a drain tide
uncovers rows of shells with plum and pearl linings.
They prodded the clusters,
twisting the plump husks, filling their buckets.

He said how few days each year
the tide pulls back this far.
Twice a month. Maybe.
Six times in a season.

She wondered
where the tidewater goes,
how far it travels, if ever
the same water comes back.

It was a day of good blues:
firm skies, slow-walking seas, following
sound. Not a whiff of fall.
Not an inkling of the rain which bleeds
red and amber from the maples.

APPRECIATION

The market's up, down, un-sustaining.
I put a little of this and that

for sale, trolling for confirmation
I have something the world wants.

This morning a pair of socks—
the penultimate option

in my portfolio—scalable form,
alluring color, rising

like the tide above my ankles,
images of sun, sea, *frangipani*

in the trees. And clouds—
positive indicators of value,

columns of equity—rising,
up the pant legs of my jeans.

ORGASM

Like a sneeze that goes unblessed,
it arrives with a tingle
and swells to a storm. In its lee

the furniture is moved
and there's light in the corner
where shadows once hung.

In the still after-storm
a window flower bends.
Dark-mannered clouds

pass over the sea to the east.

OF YOU OF ME

I gave you my word
and you gave it to her

each morning before dawn,
desperate, your search
for some thing to say,

your self-defeating resolve
for self. How could you
not know the silence you left?

You betray me
as you betrayed all your women,

lonely, syllable by syllable,
one vowel begetting the next,
each new poem in arm,

the sentiment that sloughs
off like a silk dress
and is hung the morning after

in a closet of blues and grays.

iv.

TRAIN

A train, what seemed like hours
coming towards me, across the bay,
fading and bridging
the tentative light
that separates morning
from yesterday's irreversible news.

I am switching tenses,
everything past—
the shadow-bends and hills—
now out of range. Father,
I hear you, riding the night
route named for the end of line.

Soon, we'll cross the river,
have coffee and sticky buns
and pass the lighted signs
through all the stations of morning.
We'll stop at every one.
Father, is this just the start

of my remembering?

COORDINATES

What do I remember? I remember the places
love happened; the coordinates—spring and summer—

still mornings, lupine, cut grass, tannic, and salt
water. Sun—always sun—on roads, sand, sheets.

In the afternoon—clouds. Altocumulus
over the mountains, mares' tails commuting

high above the coastal farms, stratus like a blanket
offshore, pulled over the chins of buildings.

I remember each waypoint, past its point of passing;
vaporous and irretrievable

until only the *logis* remains.
In the warehouses and vehicles, in the restaurants

with colored chalkboard menus and precious views,
in the ticking fields and homes that are no longer

home, I see love's course. What do I know of course?
Only that I love each place

I have lived. I smell it and wear it. The still air
before my arrival. The draft that eddies

once the destination recedes.

THE LONG LINE

When we met, you were pushing the long line,
every star connected to the one beside.

Dear friend, father of such kind words, light years
your voice has traveled from the shadows of your yard,

from the orange and cherimoya trees, jacaranda and jasmine,
starlets of your extended galaxy. Light breaks round

each piece of fruit, the roundness where shadow begins,
bright reflection where it avoids a place to end. I return

each word to you, the full moon so full tonight,
its reflection in the curtains beside the bed, its length

like the star trails of a conversation begun time zones away.

FULFILLMENT

My second job: moving
inventory. Boxes: *Check-In*
to *Back-Stock* to *Active.*

First-in, First-out, my mantra,
the velocity of small things

in motion—the way night moves,
gunmetal to dust, every star out
for delivery, journey unseen.

* * *

My first job: DJ
in an idling city, my office,
a room of interior windows,

no daylight, no view.
Where the music is the magic,

I was taught to speak, words
metered, a migration
of tightly-packed notes, flying

wherever they're dialed;
the almost-homing sound

of speakers miles away—
plosive purr, reconstituted
harmony, sweet unfolding blackness.

* * *

Three decades now, still
orchestrating, redirecting

the undeliverable, making
something of nothing,
the increasing velocity

of small things lost—
urgent overnights, undisclosed

addresses, manifest
destiny of the mislabeled,
Will Call of wait.

* * *

This morning word arrives,
a friend has moved on,

without so much
as a chime from my laptop or phone—
and it doesn't matter

that I've been doing the same thing
for 30 years, sending out my small, strange

offers to the world, hoping
someone will respond
two, three time zones away.

And it doesn't matter that I am 60
and have taken inventory each day

or that I have filled the mail streams
with things I touch and which confirm
the operational motions of my living

but that someone is there to receive me,
return the slip on the door,

collect the parcel on the porch,
the residual surprise still
between us like an anchorage

in a dark harbor, unopened
like the package on the chair
waiting for someone to come home
and sign their name to the night.

TIGHT

Because I had nothing I could say, I listened
to the braiding of her voice—one strand
honeyed as Missouri's water,
the other gravelly as Michigan's skies. Silt and grit
like the water of two tributaries.

I was tight and what I knew of discomfort
was a closed feeling in my back. So I went to her
studio, in the basement by the elevator—
a narrow room with exposed pipes, a cross
on the wall above. She worked me
and I felt her wide, rough hands.

She kneaded me and I needed her
kind indifference. Her repetitions
loosening each knot of memory,
but not the fist-head of its place.

PERMISSION

He could touch her
but did not expect to be heard.

She could talk
but did not expect to be touched.

And she did not expect
success of him, just commitment

to try to reach
across the bed

the piles of pillows,
worlds of broadcloth.

Once she gave him permission
to leave, to not agree or want

or bear witness
to the unmade bed

in which they made
their living, he felt

loved by relief
from expectation—

the unpressed layers which invite
and cover seamlessly—

and he learned that to grant is to love
by exception; to ask,

its own kind of submission.

GIFT

When it felt the darkest
night becomes, you
reached across the bed,
through all that blanketed us.

Your hand was a bird,
warm palm of heart, wings
of thumb and small finger
between my flightless ones.

And I thought of a man
you once told me about in Africa
who reached out to hold your hand.
The desperate hope he must have felt.

How large the room of the world
to every star must seem. Surrounded
in darkness, night years from earth,
hours from this breaking light,

the blackbirds beginning
to gather now below our window,
bleating, reaching,
pairing before flight.

SAUVAGE

After many years we arrived at the end of the world,
an island of sand and palms, part sea,
part center earth, part no man's land—an atoll
apart from the dissolving whole of our lives.
We earned our distance, the air's solitude
moving with nothing for it to sound against,
and it was beautiful the way high and distant places
become—memory from which sense seems inseparable.

And it wasn't just beautiful
in the ways we expected
but in the way there was no one other
to receive the tides and erosion and timeless procession
of evening clouds which love
to shadow its wildness.

And the feeling was thrilling and savage, together
alone on this rim of long-sought-after warmth
far from the Poles and birthing islands of ice—
a place we could not place
on any map we know

except to say, *we are here now,*
you are what I've found,
you are what makes this sea change
possible.

BENEDICTION

How could I leave? I had to know
What remains is given to flight.
Every goodbye lasts until someone turns.
The children carry the weight.

What remains is given to flight.
Cold, the space between draft words.
The children carry the weight—
Heartwood, fire, and smoke.

Cold, the space between draft words.
Blessed the blues that become
Heartwood, fire, and smoke.
The windows hang on cotton cords.

Blessed the blues that become
Something that calls in the night.
The windows hang on cotton cords
Weights in the frame below.

How could I go? I had to know
What remains is given to silence.
Every goodbye lasts until someone turns.
The children carry the weight.

NOTES

In "Aloof"—a *fake book* is a collection of musical lead sheets intended to help a performer quickly learn new songs. Each song in a fake book contains the melody line, basic chords, and sometimes lyrics—the minimal information needed by a musician to make an impromptu arrangement of a song (definition from Wikipedia).

"EBITDA"—EBITDA is a financial term used to describe a company's effective profitability, that is, "earnings before interest, taxes, depreciation and amortization."

"Train" is for my father.

"The Long Line" is for Kurt Brown.

ACKNOWLEDGMENTS

5 A.M., Alimentum, Autoliterte, Cortland Review, Miramar, and *Ploughshares.*

Special thanks to Laure-Anne Bosselaar for her guidance and friendship, Juan Felipe Herrera, Major Jackson, and Dan Gerber for their kind words and Martha Rhodes for her faith and wisdom. To Bill Evans for the transforming music I hear on the very best of days. Thanks also to my wife, Jodie, and my family for their patience and love.

Bruce Willard's poems have appeared in *5 A.M.*, *African American Review*, *Agni* Online, *Harvard Review*, *Ploughshares*, *Salamander*, NPR's *Writer's Almanac*, and numerous other publications. His first collection of poems, *Holding Ground*, was published by Four Way Books in 2013. Willard is a graduate of Middlebury College and holds a MFA from Bennington College's Writing Seminars program. He spends his time in Maine, Colorado, and California. In addition to his work as a poet, Willard currently runs *32 Bar Blues* and oversees several other clothing businesses.

Publication of this book was made possible by grants and donations. We are also grateful to those individuals who participated in our 2015 Build a Book Program. They are:

Jan Bender-Zanoni, Betsy Bonner, Deirdre Brill, Carla & Stephen Carlson,Liza Charlesworth, Catherine Degraw & Michael Connor, Greg Egan, Martha Webster & Robert Fuentes, Anthony Guetti, Hermann Hesse, Deming Holleran, Joy Jones, Katie Childs & Josh Kalscheur, Michelle King, David Lee, Howard Levy, Jillian Lewis, Juliana Lewis, Owen Lewis, Alice St. Claire Long & David Long, Catherine McArthur, Nathan McClain,Carolyn Murdoch, Tracey Orick, Kathleen Ossip, Eileen Pollack, BarbaraPreminger, Vinode Ramgopal, Roni Schotter, Soraya Shalforoosh, Marjorie& Lew Tesser, David Tze, Abby Wender, and Leah Nanako Winkler.